_____,

this is your very own special book!
It was selected for you even before you
were born. It is filled with all the important things
in your life. It is about YOU, your family, your home,
and your world. Do you remember when you were a
tiny little baby? Do you remember when you first crawled
and what your favorite first food was? What made you
laugh when you were little and what made you really, really
mad? What were your favorite games, songs, and books?
the big book of me will remind you. You'll love your
special book when you are two, and you'll love it when
you are all grown-up. Help to fill it in and record
everything from your first five years. We want this book
to show you what a special person
you are and how very
much loved you are.

5" x 7"

the big book of me

my baby book

Welcome Books

New York • San Francisco

table of contents

In Anticipation

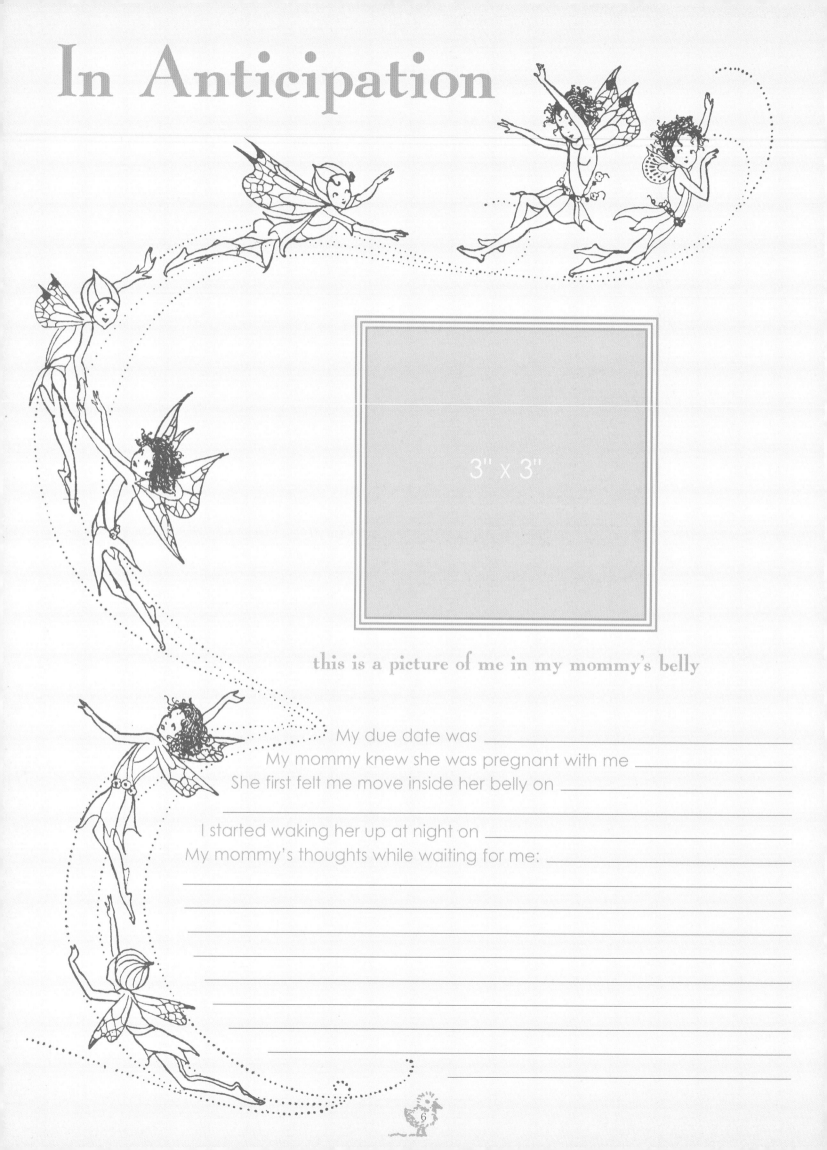

3" x 3"

this is a picture of me in my mommy's belly

My due date was _____

My mommy knew she was pregnant with me _____

She first felt me move inside her belly on _____

_____

I started waking her up at night on _____

My mommy's thoughts while waiting for me: _____

_____

_____

_____

_____

_____

_____

5" x 7"

this is my mommy with me in her belly

Life is always a rich and steady time when you are waiting for something to happen or to hatch.

—CHARLOTTE'S WEB, E. B. WHITE

My Family's History

_____
_____
_____
_____
_____
_____
_____
_____
_____
_____
_____
_____
_____
_____
_____
_____
_____
_____
_____
_____
_____
_____
_____
_____
_____
_____
_____
_____
_____
_____
_____

"If you become a bird and fly away from me," said his mother,
"I will be a tree that you come home to."

—_THE RUNAWAY BUNNY_, MARGARET WISE BROWN

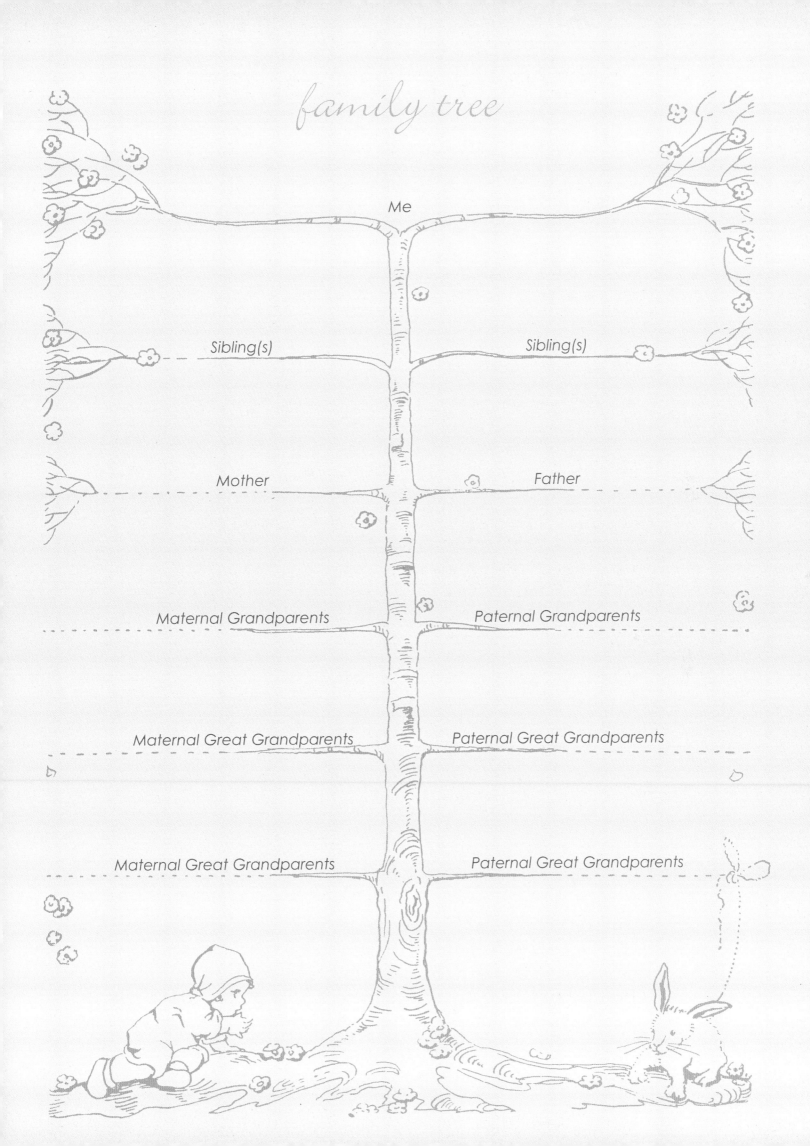

family tree

Me

Sibling(s)   Sibling(s)

Mother   Father

Maternal Grandparents   Paternal Grandparents

Maternal Great Grandparents   Paternal Great Grandparents

Maternal Great Grandparents   Paternal Great Grandparents

My Mommy & Daddy

My mommy's name is _____

She was born on _____

She was born in _____

and raised in _____

She spends her time _____

_____

_____

_____

_____

_____

_____

_____

_____

_____

Her favorite things to do are _____

_____

_____

_____

_____

_____

_____

_____

_____

_____

_____

_____

_____

_____

_____

_____

My daddy's name is _____

He was born on _____

He was born in _____

and raised in _____

He spends his time _____

_____

_____

_____

_____

_____

_____

His favorite things to do are _____

_____

_____

_____

_____

_____

_____

_____

My mommy and daddy met _____

_____

_____

_____

_____

_____

_____

_____

My Grandparents

My dad's mom's name is _____

Her birthdate is _____

She was born in _____

Her interests and hobbies: _____

_____

_____

_____

Her thoughts on being a grandmother: _____

_____

_____

_____

_____

_____

_____

My dad's dad's name is _____

His birthdate is _____

He was born in _____

His interests and hobbies: _____

_____

_____

_____

His thoughts on being a grandfather: _____

_____

_____

_____

_____

_____

How my grandparents met: _____

_____

_____

_____

*N*obody can do for little children what grandparents do.
Grandparents sort of sprinkle stardust over the lives of little children.

—ALEX HALEY

My mom's mom's name is _____

Her birthdate is _____

She was born in _____

Her interests and hobbies: _____

_____

_____

Her thoughts on being a grandmother: _____

_____

_____

_____

_____

My mom's dad's name is _____

His birthdate is _____

He was born in _____

His interests and hobbies: _____

_____

_____

His thoughts on being a grandfather: _____

_____

_____

_____

_____

How my grandparents met: _____

_____

_____

_____

_____

My Shower

It was the first party to which Roo had ever been, and he was very excited.

—WINNIE-THE-POOH, A. A. MILNE

My shower was on _____

It was given by _____

at _____

Guests	Gifts
_____	_____
_____	_____
_____	_____
_____	_____
_____	_____
_____	_____
_____	_____
_____	_____
_____	_____
_____	_____
_____	_____
_____	_____
_____	_____
_____	_____
_____	_____
_____	_____
_____	_____
_____	_____
_____	_____
_____	_____
_____	_____
_____	_____
_____	_____
_____	_____
_____	_____

Thoughts and wishes of family and friends

_____   _____
_____   _____
_____   _____
_____   _____
_____   _____
_____   _____
_____   _____
_____   _____
_____   _____
_____   _____
_____   _____
_____   _____
_____   _____
_____   _____
_____   _____
_____   _____
_____   _____
_____   _____
_____   _____
_____   _____
_____   _____
_____   _____

I Arrive!

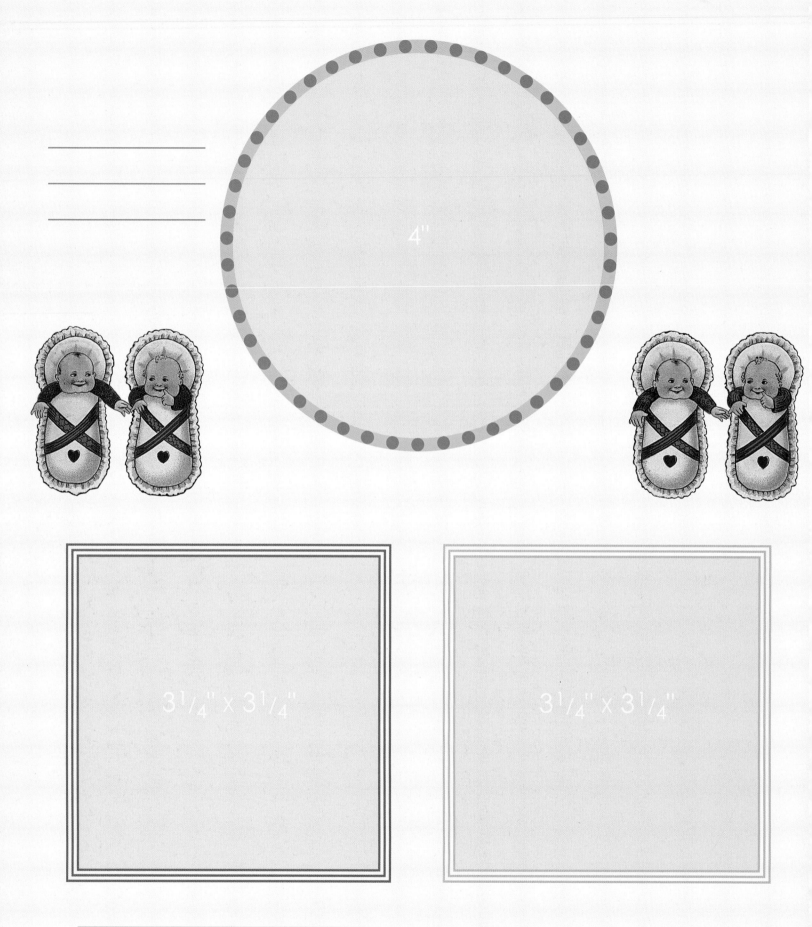

4"

3¹/₄" x 3¹/₄"   3¹/₄" x 3¹/₄"

A person's a person, no matter how small.

—DR. SEUSS

My name is _____
_____ .

I was born on _____
at _____ o'clock
in _____
_____ .

I weighed _____ .
I measured _____ in length
and _____ in head circumference.
I had _____ hair and _____ eyes
and a _____ wail.

Memories

_____
_____
_____
_____
_____
_____
_____
_____
_____
_____
_____
_____
_____
_____
_____
_____
_____
_____
_____
_____

My Baby Announcement

The first cry of a newborn baby in Chicago or Zamboango,
in Amsterdam or Rangoon, has the same pitch and key, each saying,
"I am! I have come through! I belong! I am a member of the Family!

—CARL SANDBURG

paste baby anouncement here

Predictions

And will you succeed?
Yes! You will, indeed!
(98 and 3/4 percent guaranteed.)

—*Oh, the Places You'll Go!*, Dr. Seuss

My Astrological sign is _____
Some characteristics of my sign are
_____
_____
_____
_____
_____
_____
_____
_____
_____
_____
_____
_____

My birthstone is _____

Predictions by family and friends:
_____
_____
_____
_____
_____
_____
_____
_____
_____

Little Bits of Me

I started teething on _____

I got my first tooth on _____

I got my second tooth on _____

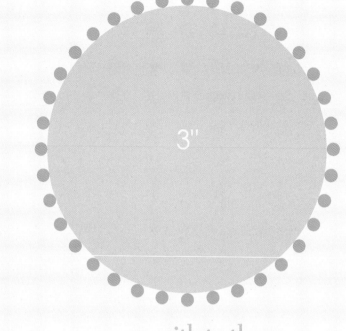

me with teeth

a lock of my hair

Everybody says my hair is just like _____

_____

_____

_____

I had my first haircut on _____

This little piggy went to market,
This little piggy stayed home,
This little piggy had roast beef,
This little piggy had none,
And this little piggy cried,
Wee, wee, wee, all the way home.

Handprints and Footprints

left hand   right hand

left foot   right foot

My World

When I was born important world events were _____
_____
_____
_____
_____

The president was _____
The music Mommy and Daddy were listening to was _____
_____

Their favorite movies and television shows were _____
_____
_____
_____

Exciting sports events were _____
_____
_____
_____

The price of things:
postage stamp _____   gasoline _____
milk _____   college _____
newspaper _____   other _____
_____
Other signs of the times were _____
_____
_____
_____
_____
_____
_____

The five little puppies dug a
hole under the fence . . .
and went for a walk in the
wide, wide world.
—*THE POKY LITTLE PUPPY*

Home

The third little pig worked from morning til night
and built himself a beautiful house of bricks.

—THE THREE LITTLE PIGS

My address is _____

_____

I live with _____

_____

The favorite things in my room are _____

_____

_____

_____

Things I love to do at home are _____

_____

_____

_____

_____

_____

_____

_____

My favorite neighborhood places and outings are _____

_____

_____

_____

_____

_____

_____

_____

_____

Record of Growth

age	weight	height
1 week		
2 weeks		
1 month		
2 months		
3 months		
5 months		
7 months		
9 months		
1 year		
18 months		
2 years		
3 years		
4 years		
5 years		

3¹/₂" x 5"

3¹/₂" x 5"

little me

medium me

3¹/₂" x 5"

big me!

My First Time

Smiling _____

Holding head up _____

Rolling over _____

Laughing _____

Sitting up _____

Eating solid food _____

Crawling _____

Standing up _____

Playing peekaboo _____

Waving bye-bye _____

Stepping _____

Talking _____

Walking _____

Climbing up stairs _____

Running _____

Humming and singing _____

Other great achievements _____

_____

_____

_____

_____

_____

_____

_____

_____

_____

_____

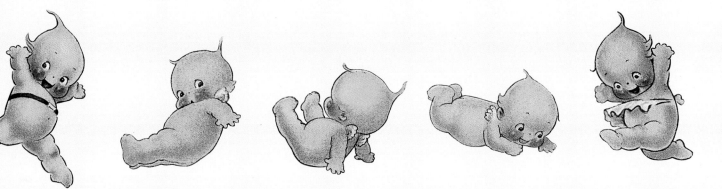

When the first baby laughed for the first time,
the laugh broke into a thousand pieces
and they all went skipping about,
and that was the beginning of fairies

—J. M. BARRIE

I smiled for the first time at _____

_____

I laughed out loud for the first time when _____

_____

My first solid food was _____

_____

I took my first steps toward _____

_____

My first words and sentences were _____

_____

_____

3¹/₂" x 3¹/₂"

3"

_____

_____

_____

_____

_____

_____

27

Sweet Dreams

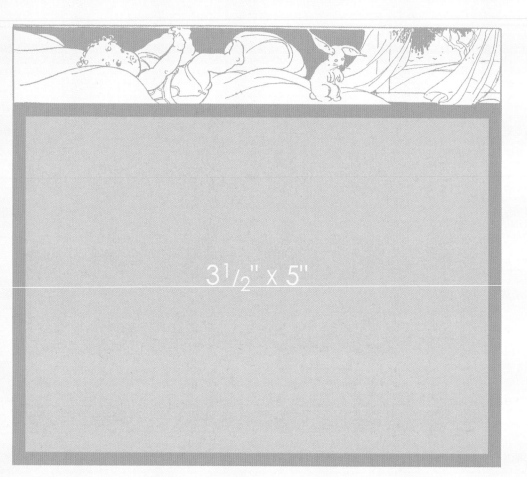

a little angel

I finally slept through the night on _____

My favorite things for bedtime are _____

_____

_____

_____

_____

_____

_____

Some of my mommy and daddy's thoughts and dreams when I was little:

_____

_____

_____

_____

_____

_____

_____

_____

_____

_____

_____

_____

_____

_____

_____

_____

_____

_____

_____

_____

_____

_____

Wynken and Blynken are two little eyes,

And Nod is a little head,

And the wooden shoe that sailed the skies

Is a wee one's trundle-bed.

So shut your eyes while mother sings

Of wonderful sights that be,

And you shall see the beautiful things

As you rock in the misty sea . . .

—EUGENE FIELD

Favorite Things

The world is so full of a number of things,
I'm sure we should all be as happy as kings.

—ROBERT LOUIS STEVENSON

My favorite toys: _____

_____

_____

My favorite games: _____

_____

_____

My favorite books: _____

_____

_____

My favorite rhymes: _____

_____

_____

My favorite television shows and videos: _____

_____

_____

Other favorite things: _____

_____

_____

_____

_____

_____

_____

3¹/₂" x 5"

3"

3"

That's Funny!

4"

Hey, diddle diddle!
The cat and the fiddle,
The cow jumped over the moon,
The little dog laughed
To see such sport,
And the dish ran away
with the spoon.

—MOTHER GOOSE

_____

_____

_____

What makes me laugh:

_____
_____
_____
_____
_____
_____
_____
_____
_____
_____
_____
_____
_____

I'm Mad!

"But I don't want to go among mad people," said Alice.
"Oh, you can't help that," said the cat. "We're all mad here."

—*ALICE'S ADVENTURES IN WONDERLAND, LEWIS CARROLL*

Things that make me sad: _____
_____
_____

Things that make me mad: _____
_____
_____

When I am mad I _____
_____
_____

I always feel better when _____
_____
_____

3½" x 5"

_____

Bathtime

Rub-a-dub-dub, three men in a tub,
The butcher, the baker, the candlestick maker.

—MOTHER GOOSE

I took my first bath on _____
My favorite water toys are _____
_____

At bathtime, I love _____
_____
_____
_____
_____

_____
_____
_____

3¹/₂" x 5"

I Love Food!

3½" x 5"

_____
_____
_____

My favorite things to eat are _____
_____
_____
_____
_____

I really don't like _____
_____
_____
_____
_____

Say! I like green eggs and ham! I do! I like them, Sam-I-am!

—GREEN EGGS AND HAM, DR. SEUSS

Musical Me

My favorite songs are _____
_____
_____
_____
_____
_____
_____

I like making music with _____
_____
_____
_____
_____
_____

The first time I danced to music _____
_____
_____
_____
_____
_____
_____

Oh, the wonderful sounds
Mr. Brown can do.
Why don't you try
to do them too?

—MR. BROWN CAN MOO! CAN YOU?,
DR. SEUSS

My Artworks

And he set off on his walk,
taking his big purple crayon with him.

—HAROLD AND THE PURPLE CRAYON,
CROCKETT JOHNSON

My first attempts at art: _____
_____
My mom's praises: _____
_____
_____

paste masterpiece here

Record of Cute Sayings

Date   Sayings

_____

_____

_____

_____

_____

_____

_____

_____

_____

_____

_____

_____

_____

_____

_____

_____

_____

_____

_____

_____

_____

_____

_____

& Sensible Remarks

Date   Sayings

_____

_____

_____

_____

_____

_____

_____

_____

_____

_____

_____

_____

_____

_____

_____

_____

"The time has come," the Walrus said,
"to talk of many things: Of shoes—
and ships—and sealing wax—
Of cabbages—and kings . . ."

—*Through the Looking Glass,*
Lewis Carroll

Mommy and Me

The favorite things I like to do with Mommy are _____

_____

_____

_____

_____

_____

_____

_____

_____

_____

4" x 6"

_____

_____

*And Max the King of all wild things was lonely
and wanted to be where someone loved him best of all.*
—*WHERE THE WILD THINGS ARE, MAURICE SENDAK*

A letter from my mommy to me

Daddy and Me

4" x 6"

HOP POP
We like to hop
We like to hop
on top of Pop.

—HOP ON POP, DR. SEUSS

The favorite things I like to do with Daddy are _____

_____

_____

_____

_____

_____

A letter from my daddy to me

_____
_____
_____
_____
_____
_____
_____
_____
_____
_____
_____
_____
_____
_____
_____
_____
_____
_____
_____
_____
_____
_____
_____
_____
_____
_____
_____
_____
_____
_____
_____
_____
_____

My Family and Me

A family is
everybody all together.

—*A Baby Sister for Frances,*
Russel Hoban

The special members of my family are _____

_____

_____

_____

_____

_____

_____

The favorite things I do with them are _____

_____

_____

_____

_____

_____

_____

_____

_____

_____

_____

_____

_____

_____

_____

_____

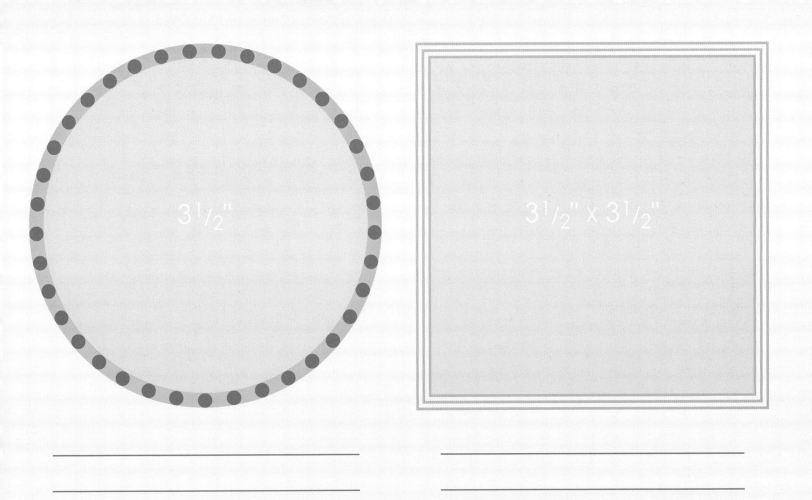

3½"

3½" x 3½"

4" x 6"

45

Best Friends

name _____
age _____
things we do _____
_____
_____
_____
_____
_____
_____
_____
_____
_____
_____
_____
_____

name _____
age _____
things we do _____
_____
_____
_____
_____
_____
_____
_____
_____
_____
_____
_____
_____

"You have been my friend. That in itself is a tremendous thing."

—*CHARLOTTE'S WEB*, E. B. WHITE

name _____
age _____
things we do _____
_____
_____
_____
_____
_____
_____
_____
_____
_____

name _____
age _____
things we do _____
_____
_____
_____
_____
_____
_____
_____
_____
_____

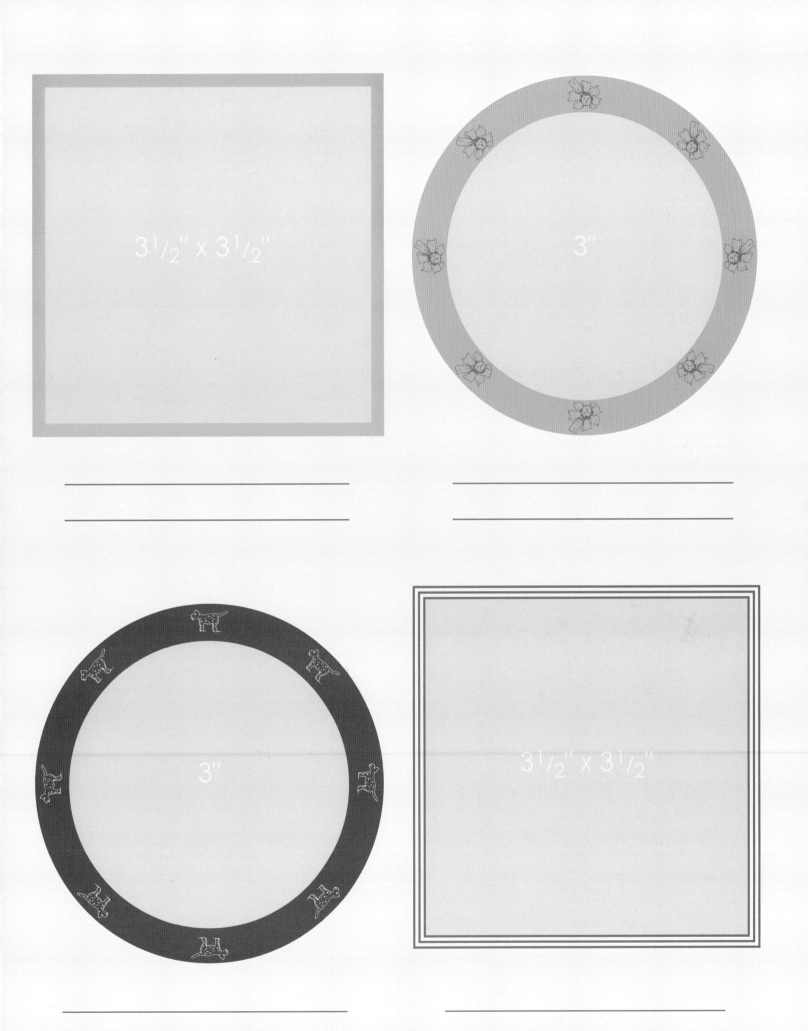

$3^1/_2" \times 3^1/_2"$

$3"$

$3"$

$3^1/_2" \times 3^1/_2"$

I Am What I Am!

When I was a year old, I had these character traits: _____
_____
_____
_____
_____
_____
_____
_____

My daddy says I remind him of _____
_____
_____
_____
_____
_____
_____
_____

My mommy says I remind her of _____
_____
_____
_____
_____
_____
_____
_____

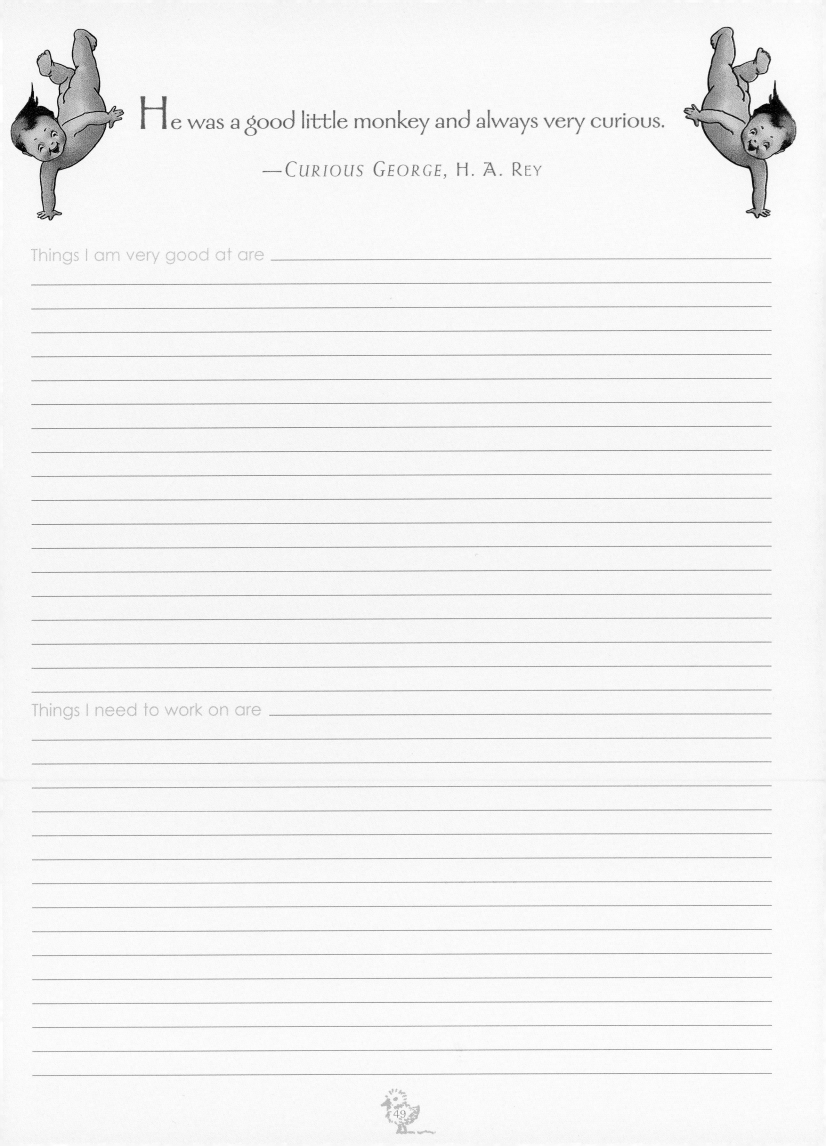

He was a good little monkey and always very curious.

—*Curious George*, H. A. Rey

Things I am very good at are _____

_____

_____

_____

_____

_____

_____

_____

_____

_____

_____

_____

_____

_____

_____

Things I need to work on are _____

_____

_____

_____

_____

_____

_____

_____

_____

_____

_____

_____

_____

_____

It's Spring

4" x 6"

The special things I do in the spring: _____
_____
_____
_____
_____
_____
_____
_____
_____
_____
_____
_____
_____

Spring is showery, flowery, bowery . . .

Summertime Fun

The fun things I do during the summer: _____
_____
_____
_____
_____
_____
_____
_____
_____
_____
_____
_____
_____
_____
_____

4" x 6"

Summer: hoppy, croppy, poppy . . .

It's Fall

The special things I do in the fall: _____

_____

_____

_____

_____

_____

_____

_____

_____

_____

_____

_____

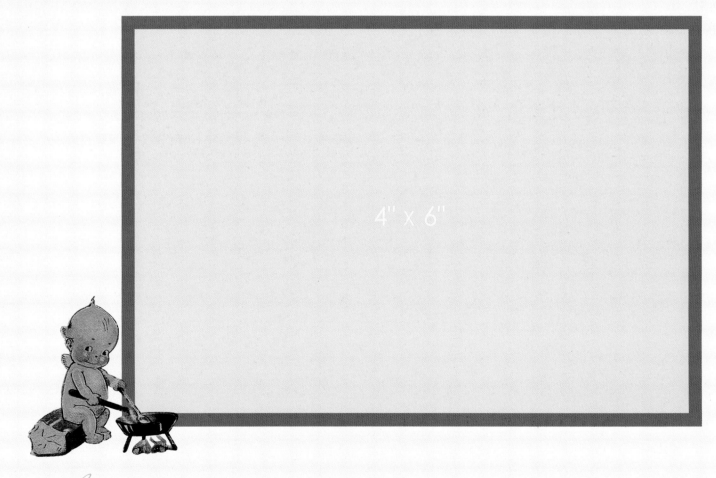

4" x 6"

Autumn: wheezy, sneezy, freezy . . .

Wintertime Fun

4" x 6"

The special things I do in the winter: _____
_____
_____
_____
_____
_____
_____
_____
_____
_____
_____
_____
_____
_____
_____
_____

Winter: slippy, drippy, nippy.
—MOTHER GOOSE

Outings

I went to the animal fair;
the birds and the beasts were there.
The big baboon by the light of the moon,
was combing his auburn hair.
The monkey, he got drunk;
he sat on the elephant's trunk.
The elephant sneezed and fell to his knees
and that was the end of the monk!

4" x 6"

_____
_____
_____
_____

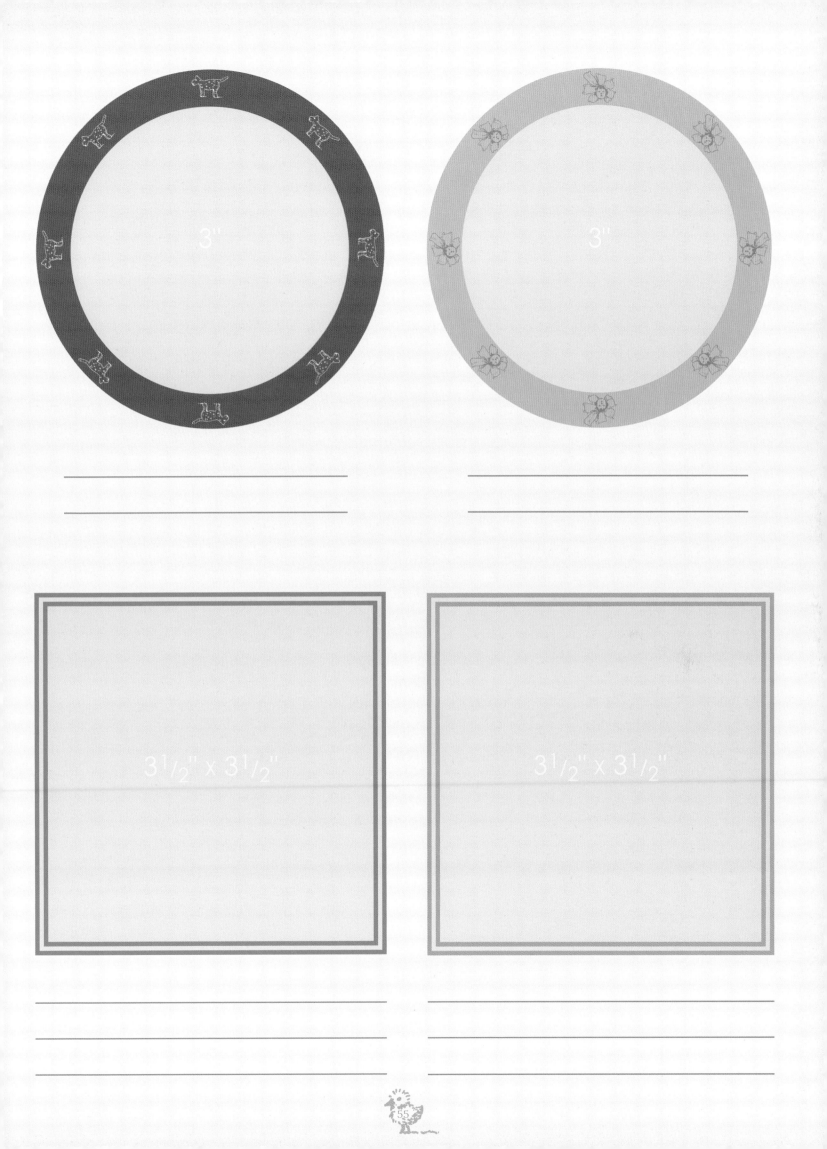

3"

3"

3¹/₂" x 3¹/₂"

3¹/₂" x 3¹/₂"

Travels

4" x 6"

_____

_____

_____

_____

_____

"Second to the right,
and straight on til morning."

—PETER PAN, J. M. BARRIE

4" X 6"

3"   3"

Travels

3" x 3"

3" x 3"

3"

3"

4" x 6"

_____

_____

_____

"I have a new space helmet.
I am going to the moon,"
said Little Bear to Mother Bear.

—*Little Bear*,
Else Holmelund Minarik

59

4" x 6"

special day: _____

memories: _____

_____

_____

_____

The guests have gone home, happy, though tired . . .
They will long remember this great celebration.

—THE STORY OF BABAR, JEAN DE BRUNHOFF

5" x 7"

special day: _____

memories: _____

_____

_____

_____

_____

Holidays & Special Events

special day: _____

_____

memories: _____

_____

_____

_____

3"

3¹/₄" x 3¹/₄"

3¹/₄" x 3¹/₄"

special day: _____

memories: _____

_____

_____

3¹⁄₂" x 5"

special day: _____

memories: _____

_____

_____

3"

3"

special day: _____

memories: _____

_____

_____

Holidays & Special Events

special day: _____

_____

memories: _____

_____

_____

_____

_____

3"

4" x 6"

special day: _____

memories: _____

_____

_____

3¹⁄₂" x 5"

special day: _____

memories: _____

_____

_____

3"

3"

special day: _____

memories: _____

_____

_____

Me, Month by Month

Date   Notes

_____

_____

_____

_____

_____

_____

_____

_____

_____

_____

_____

_____

_____

_____

_____

_____

_____

_____

_____

_____

_____

I can't go back to yesterday because I was a different person then.

—*THROUGH THE LOOKING GLASS*, LEWIS CARROLL

Date   Notes

Me, Month by Month

Date   Notes

_____

_____

_____

_____

_____

_____

_____

_____

_____

_____

_____

_____

_____

_____

_____

_____

_____

_____

_____

_____

_____

Date   Notes

_____

_____

_____

_____

_____

_____

_____

_____

_____

_____

_____

_____

_____

_____

_____

_____

_____

_____

_____

_____

_____

_____

_____

_____

_____

_____

_____

_____

_____

My First Birthday

I celebrated my first birthday on _____
_____

The party was at _____
_____
_____

My guests included _____
_____
_____
_____
_____
_____

My favorite presents were _____
_____
_____
_____
_____

I am one years old now! The amazing things I can do are _____

_____
_____
_____
_____
_____
_____
_____
_____
_____
_____
_____
_____

"It's my birthday.
The happiest day of the year."

—Eeyore, *Winnie-the-Pooh*, A. A. Milne

3½" x 3½"

3½" x 3½"

4" x 6"

I'm Two!

We celebrated my second birthday _____

_____

_____

_____

_____

I am two years old now! The amazing things I can do are _____

_____

_____

_____

_____

_____

_____

_____

4" x 6"

I'm Three!

4" x 6"

We celebrated my third birthday _____
_____
_____
_____
_____

I am three years old now! The amazing things I can do are
_____
_____
_____
_____
_____
_____
_____
_____
_____

I'm Four!

We celebrated my fourth birthday _____

_____

_____

_____

_____

I am four years old now! The amazing things I can do are

_____

_____

_____

_____

_____

_____

_____

4" x 6"

I'm Five!

All children, except one, grow up.

—PETER PAN, J. M. BARRIE

4" x 6"

We celebrated my fifth birthday _____
_____
_____
_____
_____
_____

I am five years old now! The amazing things I can do are
_____
_____
_____
_____
_____
_____
_____
_____

So Much to Remember

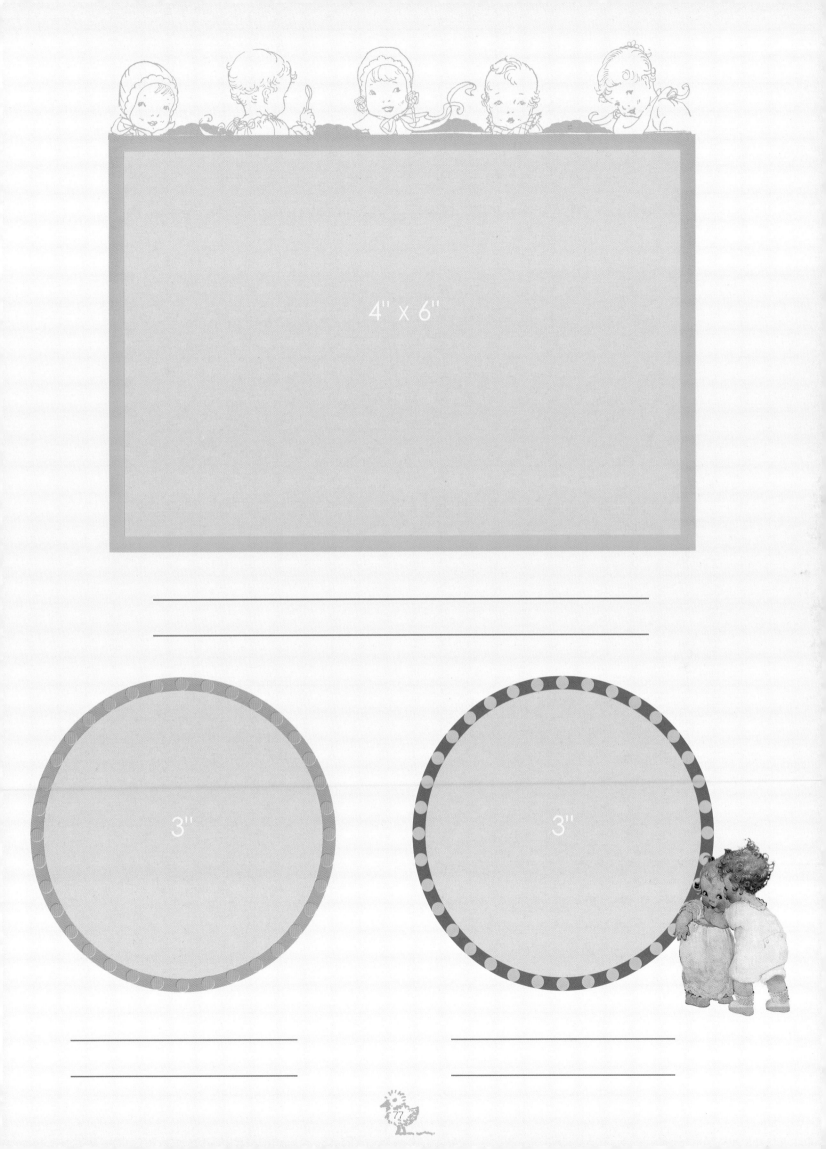

4" x 6"

3"

3"

So Much to Remember

4" x 6"

3"

Published by Welcome Books®
An imprint of Rizzoli International Publications, Inc.
300 Park Avenue South
New York, NY 10010
www.rizzoliusa.com

Text by Alice Wong
Designed by Naomi Irie

Illustrations Credits
Back cover: Hilda Austin; page 4: Edna Cooke; page 20: P. Ebner; pages 23, 26, 41, 52, 56, 69: Rosie O'neil; page 25: C. M. Burd; page 34: Pete Fraser; page 35: E. Curtis; page 46: Charlotte Becker; page 54: Margaret Evans Price; page 60: H. Q. C. Marsh; page 67: G. G. Drayton; page 73: C. Twelvetrees; page 77: Torre Bevans.

Library of Congress Cataloging-in-Publication Data on file.

ISBN: 978-1-59962-070-1

Printed in China

2015 2016 2017 2018 / 10 9 8 7 6 5

I kiss you and kiss you,
With arms 'round my own,
Ah, how shall I miss you,
When, dear, you have grown.

—WILLIAM BUTLER YEATS